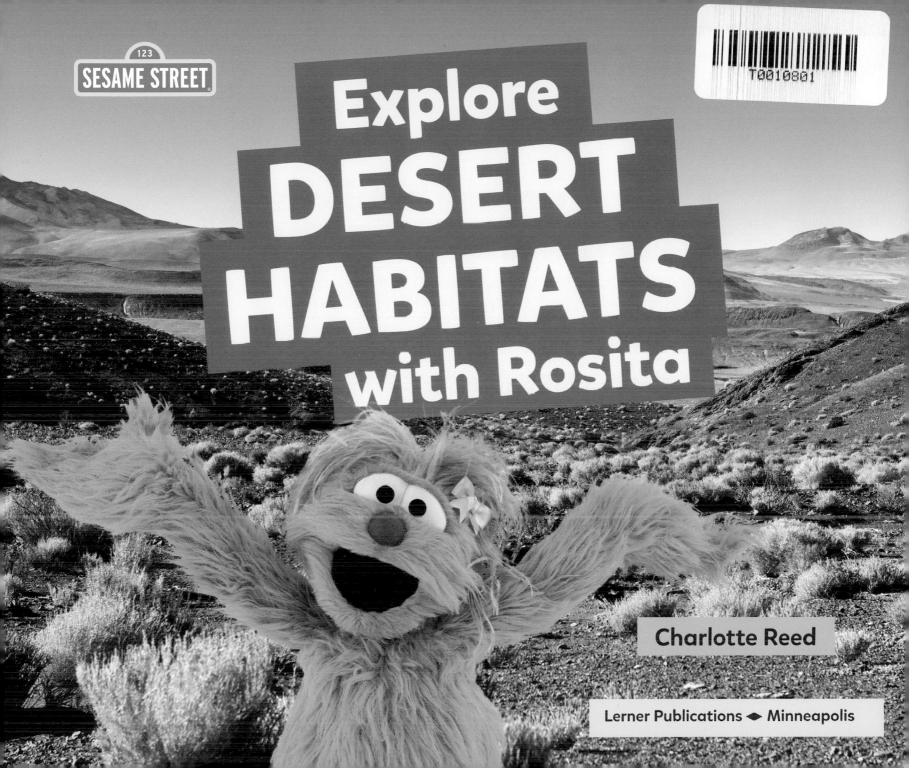

Explore DESERT HABITATS with Rosita

Charlotte Reed

Lerner Publications ◆ Minneapolis

There are many habitats to explore!

In the Sesame Street® Habitats series, young readers will take a tour of eight habitats. Join your friends from *Sesame Street* as they learn about these different habitats where animals live, sleep, and find food and water.

Sincerely,
The Editors at Sesame Workshop

Table of Contents

WHAT IS A HABITAT?

Let's explore habitats! A habitat is a place where animals live, sleep, and find food and water. A desert habitat is a type of habitat.

Let's learn about deserts!

Plants such as the prickly pear cactus and the Joshua tree can be found in the desert.

Many kinds of animals live there too.

Elmo can't wait to learn more about desert animals!

LET'S LOOK AT DESERT HABITATS

Many deserts have very hot days all year long. Desert animals still find food, water, and a place to sleep.

There are a lot of sunny days in the desert.

Avoiding the sun helps some animals stay cool during the day. This sand viper buries itself in the sand to stay cool.

The desert is cooler at night when the sun is down.

Some animals are nocturnal. That means they sleep during the hot day and stay awake during the cool night.

Me not nocturnal. Me sleep at night.

Fennec foxes are nocturnal. They sleep during the day and look for food at night.

These foxes are just starting to wake up when it's my bedtime!

Deserts are very dry. It doesn't rain a lot in the desert.

I will not be needing this umbrella.

A cactus is a type of desert plant. It has a thick stem that stores water when it rains.

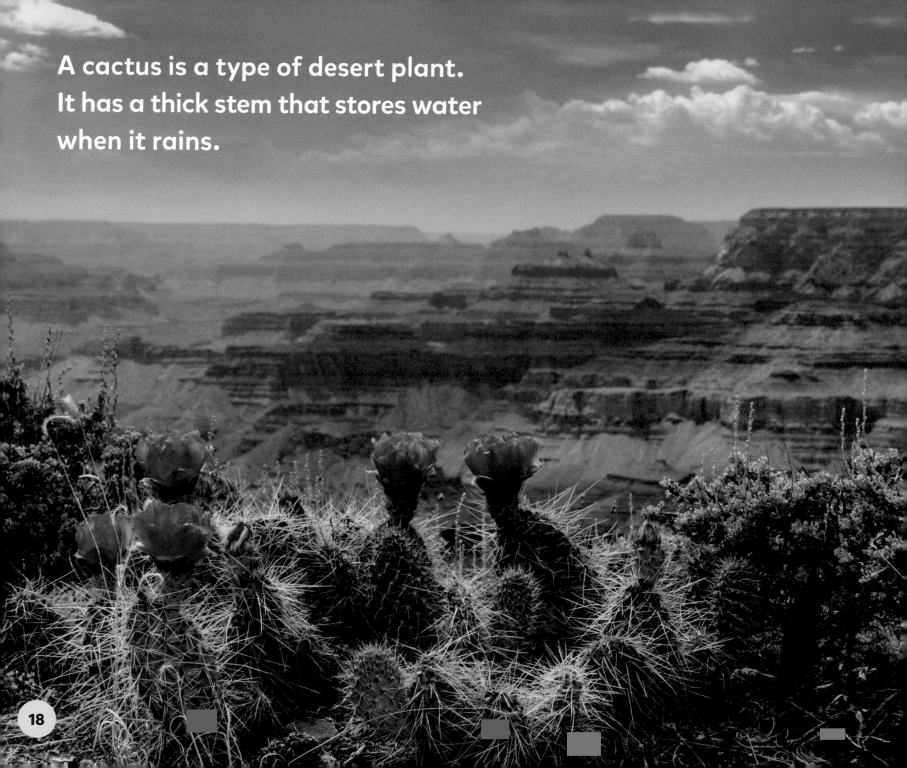

The aloe vera plant is another type of desert plant.

The aloe vera plant stores water too!

An Arabian oryx can go weeks without drinking water.

During that time, it gets water by eating plants.

That's a long time to go without water!

Because the desert is dry, some animals don't take baths in water. The kangaroo rat takes dust baths to keep its fur healthy.

Some deserts are very sandy. Camels have long eyelashes to keep sand from blowing into their eyes.

Their eyelashes look like mine.

Desert habitats are found all over the world. Deserts are home to these animals and many more!

There is so much
to explore!

27

CAN YOU GUESS?

1. Which one of these pictures is of a desert habitat?

A

B

2. Which one of these animals lives in a desert?

A

B

Glossary

dust baths: when animals roll in the dirt, dust, or sand to clean themselves

habitat: a place where animals live and can find water, food, and a place to sleep

nocturnal: an animal that is awake at night and sleeps during the day

stem: the part of a cactus that stores water

Can You Guess? Answers

1. B
2. A

Read More

Peters, Katie. *Animals in the Hot Desert*. Minneapolis: Lerner Publications, 2020.

Reed, Charlotte. *Explore Polar Habitats with Ernie*. Minneapolis: Lerner Publications, 2024.

Weglinski, Michaela. *In the Desert*. Washington, DC: National Geographic Kids, 2020.

Photo Acknowledgments

Image credits: Antonio Busiello/Moment/Getty Images, p. 1; Andrea Paganini Photo/iStock/Getty Images, p. 5; Daniela Duncan/Moment/Getty Images, p. 6; Marco Ossino/Shutterstock, p. 6 (circle); R.M. Nunes/iStock/Getty Images, p. 9; Mark Kostich/iStock/Getty Images, p. 10; David ODell/Shutterstock, p. 12; Steve-K/iStock/Getty Images, p. 14; Wirestock/iStock/Getty Images, p. 15; OlyaSolodenko/iStock/Getty Images, p. 17; DGHayes/iStock/Getty Images, p. 18; Chichimaru/Shutterstock, p. 19; Carlene Thurston/iStock/Getty Images, p. 20; Yerbolat Shadrakhov/iStock/Getty Images, p. 22; Nurdin Nurdin/EyeEm/Getty Images, pp. 24, 25; Anywhere We Roam/iStock/Getty Images, p. 26 (ostrich); MikeLane45/iStock/Getty Images, p. 26 (roadrunner); fotoclick/E+/Getty Images, p. 26 (chameleon); Francesco Riccardo Iacomino/Moment/Getty Images, p. 28 (rainforest); sprokop/iStock/Getty Images, p. 28 (desert); tzooka/iStock/Getty Images, p. 29 (fennec fox); Andre Pinto/ /Getty Images, p. 29 (alligator).

Front cover: janetteasche/RooM/Getty Images; Ondrej Prosicky/iStock/Getty Images (oryx).
Back cover: Chichimaru/Shutterstock (aloe vera); ali suliman/iStock/Getty Images (camel).

Index

For Stephanie, my kind sister and fellow desert baby

Lerner Publications Company
An imprint of Lerner Publishing Group, Inc.
241 First Avenue North
Minneapolis, MN 55401 USA

For reading levels and more information, look up this title at www.lernerbooks.com.

Main body text set in Mikado provided by HVD.

Editor: Amber Ross **Designer:** Laura Otto Rinne

Library of Congress Cataloging-in-Publication Data

Names: Reed, Charlotte, 1997– author.
Title: Explore desert habitats with Rosita / Charlotte Reed.
Description: Minneapolis : Lerner Publications, [2024] | Series: Sesame Street habitats | Includes bibliographical references and index. | Audience: Ages 4–8 | Audience: Grades K–1 | Summary: "Not all animals can survive in a hot, dry desert. Join Rosita and her Sesame Street friends as they explore a desert habitat"– Provided by publisher.
Identifiers: LCCN 2023004533 (print) | LCCN 2023004534 (ebook) | ISBN 9798765604212 (lib. bdg.) | ISBN 9798765617427 (epub)
Subjects: LCSH: Desert animals—Habitations—Juvenile literature. | Desert ecology—Juvenile literature. | BISAC: JUVENILE NONFICTION / Science & Nature / Environmental Science & Ecosystems
Classification: LCC QL116 .R44 2024 (print) | LCC QL116 (ebook) | DDC 591.754—dc23/eng/20230421

LC record available at https://lccn.loc.gov/2023004533
LC ebook record available at https://lccn.loc.gov/2023004534

Manufactured in the United States of America
1-1009512-51408-4/27/2023